BRAIN CAMP

Pitt Poetry Series

Ed Ochester, Editor

BRAIN CAMP

CHARLES HARPER WEBB

University of Pittsburgh Press

Published by the University of Pittsburgh Press, Pittsburgh, Pa., 15260
Copyright © 2015, Charles Harper Webb

10 9 8 7 6 5 4 3 2 1
ISBN 13: 978-0-8229-6338-7
ISBN 10: 0-8229-6338-8

for Karen and Erik

CONTENTS

PART III

DEDICATION

Where did Blake Bumgardner find the washtub-sized
cojones to confess over the phone, then listen
        as K I L T's Big Bass Man rumbled, "This goes out
from Blake to Pam: now and forever My True Love,"

the bare-bum truth flashing past Pam, her friends,
his friends, and every living soul in Houston, before ripping
        at light speed across Texas and the whole earth, then
into space to ring out, as the song said, for "all eternity"?

How could anyone survive hearing his name publicly
linked with one he moaned to his pillow as Rosie
        & the Originals nostrilled "Angel Baby" just for her?
I quaked through Hours of Dedications, almost as afraid

that fame would flash to me from heavenly Kimi
Kidsen, as from Lynn Lonnis of the food-clogged braces,
        who slogged through Nerd Hell with me every day.
But no, the airways never had to heft my name.

Big Bass Man rocks, today, with Jed the Fish
and Charlie Tuna under death's anonymous waves.
        Huggy Boy, the last great dedicator, poofs his toupee
in a Nursing Home. The girls who steamed my dreams

are mired in menopause. Still, their memory makes
my heart flash hot. Hey Little Darlin's—Kimi,
        Sherry Baby, Suzi Q, Good Golly Miss Molly,
this one's from Charlie: Cha-Cha-Charlie, Hot-Time

Charlie Ching-Ching-Ching (that's money, honey)—
you heartbreakers, shakers of your moolah-makers
        that will never spread or sag, life's too short now
for "Maybe, baby." This goes out from me to you.

PART I

MOTH

The soul, as we know, is a gray moth
at the center of the brain. When we're awake,

it sleeps, which makes some people think
it isn't there. When we sleep, though, it leaves us

through an ear. The things it sees,
the thoughts it has outside, are *dreams*.

Once, during a World Series game,
a lost soul slipped into the pitcher's ear.

Unable to choose what pitch to throw,
he dropped onto the mound, clawing his head,

and had to be sedated until—as doctors tried
to bat it down—the soul fluttered away.

Sometimes two souls fly together for a while.
The owners say they are *in love*; they say,

soul mates. Sometimes these mates may
lose each other in the dark or, for some reason,

fly together no more. Then the two people
feel sad, though one always feels sadder.

When we die, the soul waits until no one's
looking, then flies out the least obvious ear—

not to heaven, only to the nearest
tree, where it settles on a leaf (if there aren't

leaves, a twig will do), and seeps inside.
This is why children rake leaves into mountains

> to slide down, and why men fire up
> a pile of leaves on a cold day, and stare

into the blaze, and will say only, "I like
the smell." "I like the heat." "I like the light."

WINTER SONG

After a summer that sipped iced tea on my lawn
past Halloween, then a fall that barely unpacked
its bags, and then was gone, winter's arrived
like my new son, shaking fists and blustering.

Dadhood's hard work; but so was slogging
through each hour, pushing my extinction
like a big, stalled car. When I push my boy's
blue stroller now, he magically pulls me.

Even dirty diapers lighten my load. Of course
he can't stop Age from trying to smother me.
That's why I run outside to seize more oxygen.
The wind is generous; it showers me with leaves.

Its burly shoulders roll trashcans around the yard
as I pluck up the golden fruit blown off
our bucking guava tree. My goosebumps stand
and praise the cold. The wind helps me.

My city's slanty angle to the sun helps me.
My son helps me to see: What looked
like knife-edged cliffs are bunny slopes
I ski down easily. What felt like freezing

turns warm after a while. What felt like fear
is just anticipation. Pain is foreplay to pleasure.
Nothingness is Something New. Death will be
the earth's arms reaching out to cradle me.

THANKS AGAIN

for Y.K.

to you, girl in the blue Mercedes. If I hadn't drifted
left, toward you, the blue-gray blur that sideswiped me
    on the right—a jolt, a sound like a milk carton dropped
from a height, a gouge the length of my Volkswagen bug—might

have flipped me like a turtle, or shoved me under a bus.
Thanks, also, to Motorhead; your CD speed-metaled me up
    just enough that, when the SUV ran the red at Jefferson,
it T-boned my pickup's bed, totaling my truck, not me.

Thanks to the cars lined up between mine and the drunk's
white van that, doing 80, slammed into us—all stopped
    at a light—shoving me into the intersection where, thanks
to many other drivers, none hit me. Three gangbangers

from Reagan High who threatened to *chinga* Rudy's mom—
thank you for being hard to find the night Rudy and I prowled
    Houston's streets the way our pals patrolled jungles
in Vietnam, where—many thanks, Asthma—I never had to go.

Thanks to my reflexes the day, on the 101, I watched
a dropped muffler—clipped by a big rig—rise and hover
    like a UFO until I realized it was whizzing right at me.
I swerved, then BLAM!—the thing knocked off my side

mirror as cleanly as that artillery shell clipped Bobby
Hillendahl's left hand, which spun away (he told me)
    like a ceiling fan. Thanks to some guy (I want to think
it was a guy) for eating light the night before the remnants

of his meal dropped from a plane at 20,000 feet, froze
in the sky, and slammed my Honda Civic like a meteor.

That's the one way I can explain it: my wife and I driving
home—open highway, cave-black woods on either side,

no other car in sight, when, WHAM!—as if a huge hand
had slammed down. No blood, no feathers, no rock fragments
or pinecones when we pulled over. Just a dented roof,
and a familiar smell.

EXPLANATIONS

The sun as God's eye; yolk of the sky-bird's egg;
gold vagina giving birth to day—all seem more
likely than a ball of hydrogen fusing, at fifteen
million degrees, ninety-three million miles away.

Would we say, if we'd never heard of gravity,
The apple falls when Earth calls her child home?
Would we see stones as wingless birds
that fly downhill, and can be coaxed to kill?

One war, one plague, and we may kneel again to those
who swear that rivers freeze when water sprites
hug tight for warmth; that ice-warriors kill plants
each fall, but prayers can rout the Troops of Cold.

Some *prophet* will, of course, decree, "God
wants your blood!" Still, when Science sinks
back into the unknown, we may be happy to believe
the dead shed bodies the way snakes shed skins,

and flowers are their way to say, "We still live,
full of love for you." If fire is sunlight trapped
in trees, and raindrops are plant spirits rushing
to be born, it will be clear that the soul inhabits

its skull as the turtle its shell, peering out
with bright orange eyes at cloud-cloaked mountains
where gods gather by campfires
to tell the stories that become our lives.

RESPECT

Last night, sensing the signs, Australia's long-
time light-welterweight champ Kostya Tszyu
threw in the towel on his last title fight

before he needed it to sop his brains.
Ten rounds he held off Ricky Hatton—nine years
younger, nine years hungrier—not subject,

it seemed, to the fatigue that hung water
balloons from Kostya's muscles, making even
his face droop as Hatton's punches crossed

his eyes. He'd felt his gold belt unbuckling
two rounds before, his punches falling short,
his will to battle, body-pummeled out.

In chess, it's noble to resign when hope is gone.
But Roberto "*Manos de Piedra*" Duran
never recovered from "*No mas.*" Fans groaned

when Benny "Kid" Paret died in the ring, but
they were proud of him. We picture Ali, jaw
broken, battling on; and when we see him now,

a living bobblehead, we say, "*There* was
a champion." So, though the post-fight wrap-up
credits Tszyu with a dash to the hospital

that "caught his cerebral swelling just in time,"
Hatton springs less high in victory than if Tszyu lay
convulsing. The old champ's record seems less

lustrous now, his knockouts less stunning,
challengers pounded down to journeymen
like Ruben Contreras—in his "third week of coma,"

states the Times. Ruben, who wouldn't quit
till he was carried from the ring, and who will end
his life (with luck, soon) in a nursing home,

having earned, along with brain damage,
what he never had while making other men look
good.

AMERICAN DREAM

> Why couldn't it be true?
> —Victim of a Nigerian Scam

Mariam Abacha am I, widow of General Sani Abacha,
      Nigeria Military Head of State who die mysteriously
of Cardiac Unrest. Since then, is molest my family
      by police, Bank Accounts froze, five-year son held
for interrogation is. (You have heard of Nigerian Giraffe?
      Mbutu BooBoo? You don't want, believe me.)

I am 23, with large pillows on slender chaise, but have no
      lie-down life for years. I M Adventurous, R U?
When husband's Swiss Bank Account discovered was,
      I am moved sum of 50 Million cash in Metal Boxes two.
I bleat, Religiously, for help escape money and me.
      Sunset here is violet, gold, cobalt, crimson, topaz blue

as eye shadow over jungle's emerald green, but is not
      bitchin USA. I read about on Google day and day.
No pink hyena there, or kinky jackal (torture-man, I mean)!
      E-mail phone number plus address and whole name,
please. No do not send to Samson Malolo, Esq.,
      attorney for R. Akueze, with thousand *Assalamualaikum*,

or any African who beg in fake bad English. Never write
      to Paul Rhodes, white Zimbabwean who call you *Pard*,
and say farm going seize by crazy Black, or either
      Salim Ibrahim, dying merchant of Dubai say he need be
generous so not reborn as slug or other squirmy thing.
      These guy will flimflam crud off teeth, wax out you ears.

I M Real Deal, Genuine McMuffin. Don't get took.
      You bust bum-bum all day, for what? Movie star won't
go out with! Country club don't let you in! You happy
      go to goo-head school, degree Poo-Poo Appreciation?
Want to die thinking *Washout, No-Go, All Puff No Pastry,*
      Failure is the name of me? If so, go do. Get over with.

If not, Reply. Do not tell friend. They laugh, then write
      behind your behind. Get bimp-bomp and bucks for free.
I beg you, be sincere like me. I want no gold digger
      who dump me later. Say so, please, if are you. Why be scare-
cat or cynic fatty? My goods NOT too good to be true!
      Trust someone in this viper life you got to. I pick you.

POSTMODERNISM MISSED THE OPRY

If old George sings, "I'll love you till I die,"
he isn't kidding; call a hearse. If Dolly begs
some redhead, "Please don't take my man,"
or swears, "I will always love you"—even if

you doubt her dirigible breasts, her yellow
hair high as the Tower of Babel, you know
her love is true as water's wet, sun's hot,
and dandelions whirligig on a spring day.

You know the mockingbird that trills,
Shree! Shree! Shree! Shree! while bouncing
in your apple tree, was not sent by the IRS.
Tax is a bad word in Country. Crawfish

pie is good—and barbecue, so sweet
your taste buds' friendly flowers
wiggle their vermilion heads for joy.
Irony is what a smith beats into horseshoes;

how moms smooth their family's clothes.
Aesthetic distance is the valley between
mountains full of deer, trout, bobwhites,
and the pine-shaded shack where you were born.

Postmodern is a city boy who's never been
so lonesome he could cry—who'd never
walk the line, sigh, "Hello, walls," or waltz
across Texas—who thinks he's too smart

to place a rose from her own garden on the grave
of his wife of fifty years—who hides,
in an ice chest that should be full of longnecks,
his really and truly cold, cold heart.

SOMEONE ELSE'S LIFE

What if, when you die, someone else's life
flashes before your eyes?
            —Overheard

The day after announcing he has AIDS, Freddie lies,
foggy with meds, letting Jimmy stroke his hair.
His bed feels like a quiet stream on which he drifts
toward gates of gold. On the bank, a pale boy,
dressed in what the Yanks call *dungarees*, trades
a farmer two roosters with crests like flame, and takes
a banjo from the farmer's hand. *When was this?*
Freddie thinks, watching the boy—grown tall
and thin, with big ears and a mournful face—play
that banjo on a dusty stage as people stomp and cheer.
Then he's pitching—not cricket; American baseball!
Batters slink back to their bench, shaking their heads.
Everybody calls him *Dave* until, on stage, a man
in a cowboy hat announces, "my good friend String Bean."
He's on the Grand Ole Opry in a wilted, half-sized
hat and child's blue jeans stitched to a shirt so long
he looks like a worm-man with tiny legs that wiggle
when he strums. "Run little rabbit, run, run,
yonder come a man with a big shotgun," he sings,
hands a blur on the banjo. Dressed as a scarecrow
in a field, he jokes with a man-sized crow. Now
he's marrying *Estelle*. Shooting an eight-point buck.
Hoisting a big bass from a lake close to the cabin
where he lives. Stashing cash behind a chimney brick.
Estelle drives his blue Cadillac home from the Opry.
An old Ford squats in their drive. Their front door
gapes. Two men turn as he runs in. "What the shit?"
One lifts a pistol and blasts him in the chest. He hits

the floor. "Sumbitch shot me," he thinks. It hurts
like all hell, then goes numb. The room turns
dark, as if night is flowing in, him hunkered in his boat,
casting a popper to a monster rise.

But he's sure not
in Tennessee. He's sees flowering vines, monkeys
in the trees, and brown people in funny clothes.
He's kind of small, with big, buck teeth. Farrokh,
his friends call him, speaking a strange language
he somehow understands. He's in a fancy school
where everyone's dark-skinned. He's in a boxing ring,
left-hooking a tall boy as kids with English accents
yell, "Get him, Freddie." He's drawing trees,
people, clothes, not to goof off—as part of school.
He's selling ruffled shirts in "Kensington," and playing
piano for *The Hectics*. Now, in tight pants, hair
long as a girl's, he fronts a band—the drums
say *Queen*—with harmonies Bill Monroe
would have loved. The guitar sings like a violin.
He lives with Mary, and loves her, but not for sex.
"I'm gay as a daffodil, my dear," he trills. And
it's okay. Queen makes records, and plays in stadiums
where thousands roar, "We will, we will rock you."
Now a sad-looking doctor sighs, "I have bad news."
He's thin, tired all the time, but still sings like an angel.
He trades rings with Jim Hutton, and writes, "Who
Wants to Live Forever?" He pretends that nothing's
wrong. But the gold gate starts to close. He hears
a banjo, his voice singing "We Are the Champions,"
which sounds, somehow, like "Little Liza Jane."

DAIRY FARM

When Dad lost his job and, three months
later, drove our cat family to you,
I didn't cry, holding Dad's picture
of a white-haired farmer on his stool,
squirting milk straight from the cow
to a cat's mouth as kittens, pursued
by a giggling pooch, chased
grinning mice through fragrant hay.

That same year, three of my friends' pets
went to the farm—big as the King Ranch
I supposed, with enough cows to feed
a million cats, who'd entertain a million
dogs, the farmer pushing through a crush
of loving fur that stretched for miles.

By 12, I despised any man who'd sink
a sack of cats in White Oak Bayou,
then lie. So, when my son's Miss Kitty
is crushed by a truck, I resolve, once I get
home from "the vet," to say, "She died."

But when—after I've laid Miss K to rest
in Colonel Sanders's dumpster, and killed
enough time at the news stand
to make it to and from a vet on Mars—
my boy's still sobbing, I invoke the farm.

"Miss Kitty will have all the milk she wants,
and lots of mice to chase. Then,
when she's well, if the farmer
can spare her, she'll come back here."

"It's like heaven," my son says, and dries
his tears.

THINGS WE KNOW

When Edna goes to church, her head goes with her.
—Stephen Pinker, *How the Mind Works*

When Jane's hair waves in the wind, we don't need to shout,
    "Goodbye!"
When Jim, painting his house, slops Evening Azure on his face,
    he is still Jim.
When Scylla shuts a book, the words all stay inside.

When Gladys stomps an ant, no smoke bomb triggers—no thrash-
    metal take on "Silent Night."
When Glinda boils a baby-bottle, her heart isn't burned; the good
    bacteria in her guts don't die.
When Sam picks up his morning *Times*, the lawn stays down.

Grass will rebound when we walk on it, but won't "work the trauma
    through" in therapy.
A hedge, badly trimmed, won't demand its money back.
Turtles we find crawling across a busy road will not turn into
    terrorists or legs of lamb.

If Pastor blesses the corned beef, the cow won't care.
If Jake grows up, his heart and lungs will too.
It does no good to shake his crib and dump out his old chest of
    drawers; the baby is no longer there.

When we drive to a new town, the town won't run the other way.
When we make love, we don't need more closet space for it.
Because we made it yesterday, and haven't had it since, doesn't
    mean there's any left today.

WHY ARE PEOPLE SO MEAN?

—Erik, age 6

Bad DNA? Dyslexic genes?
Forceps-dents in the brain? Earthquake
in the Library of Chromosomes,
the books reshelved by chimpanzees?

The porky teen grabs Erik's lunch, and pokes
his chest. "Do somethin' about it, kid . . . "
The tourists give up wallets, watches, rings
as asked; the pirates shoot them anyway.

Birth-cord garroting? Toxic waste
in the Neurotransmitter Sea?
Collapsed synaptic bridges?
Global warming of the hemispheres?

First day of seventh grade, Lonnie Golden—
ping-pong-paddle ears, breath like a cat box—
whangs a locker door against my head.
"Go lick your momma's sugar tit," he jeers.

Smut, rust, and blight in the gardens of empathy?
Bark beetles in good humor's tree?
Mengele-God, replacing blood with spleen?
The milk of kindness curdled to stinky cheese?

"Rita, Rita, looks like a mosquita,"
the turned-up noses tell the pointy one.
"Try this candy," the big girl sneers, and dumps
dog-doo in Jenny's sack of trick-or-treats.

Advent of the Übermensch? Alpha attack?
Big boss he come? Selfish gene?
Winner take all? Evolution's engine
crushing the slow, lame, crooked, cracked?

The tackler strips the tailback's ball.
Machete-men hack hands and feet.
Twin Towers fall. Sherman's troops
march—burning, burning—to the sea.

USE OF FORCE

after *Four Brothers*

Once, a bump in a packed hall, a grin at the wrong girl,
a single application of *Poltroon!* could set it free.
Now Law has seized a force-monopoly. Yet even pacifists

long (secretly) to Shock-and-Awe their enemies
with a nose-flattening Stink-Face, then hoist them high
for the neck-cracking, skull-shattering Tombstone Drop.

How we'd adore to give the poltroons that attacked us,
or might, a tangy taste of Atom Bomb. It's not only murderers
we want to force-feed just desserts, with a mountain of butt-

whipping cream—not only burglars, rapists, muggers,
robbers, armed or otherwise. It's asset-sucking CEOs,
public servants who serve themselves, every crooked judge

and fool-who-rules. It's bankers who squeak *remit*,
lawyers who strut poolside, flexing swollen fees.
It's purse-snatchers, snatch-pursers, cutters in checkout lines.

It's the bag-hag who blocks the crosswalk, the mom
who hogs two parking spots, the wide-beamed receptionist
who yanks the last Krispy Kreme from our thin hands.

We're born with pissed-off DNA, starved for payback,
incensed that our genes withheld the height, big breasts,
IQ, titanium jawline we deserved—that we decay and die

while God has blown away like angel dust, and our welfare's
not on Chance's (lack of) mind. Therefore, when thugs
shotgun Mother Theresa of the Hood, we cheer

to see her four sons gut the perps. When, trapped a mile
out on Lake Michigan ice, King Gangsta taunts,
"Who's got the gonads to put his hands on me?"

we hoot with glee as Momma's baddest boy—who doused
a councilman with gas, and blew cigar smoke
in his face until he ratted out the King; who, banished

from pro hockey as too violent, used chunks of drywall
to ablate a hit man's brain—stomps, now, across the frozen
lake, sucks up the King's slickest one-two, and grins.

When—kidney-punched, ball-kicked, throat-chopped—
the King is stretched like a fresh salmon on the ice
beside a hole his minions sawed—when Baddest Bro barks,

"Throw him in," knowing the hole will freeze,
the corpse never be found—we angels cheer,
in our comfy chairs, to feel so near yet be so far from sin.

BREATHALYZER

We all crave the quick fix: garlic for vampires;
rabbit's foot to kick our luck into the black.
So, when you've gulped an extra glass
of wine, or swigged too much of Jack's

Tennessee best, and—damn it all!—
a taillight fails, and a cop car screams up,
you may recall a tale you heard years ago
in high school gym, and suck a penny

to thwart the cursed device meant
to snare career blottos, not good drivers
like you. If they're handy, you may
wolf raw potatoes, peanut butter, celery—

or pound down Listerine, Binaca, TicTacs,
Clorets, Diet Coke, Icebreakers Gum,
or in England, Breathalyzer Blitz, trying
to stop your body from ratting on you.

Empty-handed, you might even,
as one desperate drunk did, tear off
and swallow strips of your skivvies,
hoping the cloth absorbs the booze.

As for the three-time loser who—
in a holding tank, watching his life cave in,
his last chance funnel down the reeking
loo—ate his own shit, convinced

the stink would flummox the machine?
"I'd never stoop that low," we think
as we slink out of a meeting with the boss,
rubbing something sticky on our chin.

IN THE FACE, HARD

A child kneels by a "dead" bee.
(Stinging black-and-gold soldier,
        where's your buzzing bluster now?)
Jab!—boxing glove in the face, hard.

A woman bends to change the diaper
on her newborn son. Whizz!—
        liquid boxing glove in the face, hard!
And before that, when, wife-to-be,

        she showed her "diamond" to a friend's
jeweler brother-in-law. Prump!—
        on a spring, stashed behind a trap door:
boxing glove in the face, very hard.

The asthmatic sniffs a perfect purple
rose; the fisherman lifts—out
        of season, right under a warden's nose—
a red, green, gold, and silver trout;

        the widow spades her spore-filled soil;
the child lowers his head to cuddle
        Tuffy the pit bull . . . boxing glove
in the face, extremely hard!

This is why the baby howls and bites
the breast—why the old ones rest
        in wheelchairs, staring into space,
terror on each toothless, smashed-in face.

HOW CAN I EXCEED YOUR EXPECTATIONS?

—Bank employee, answering the phone

Cut earth's human population two-thirds, without being mean.
Credit ten million to my account as compensation for your lamprey-
     fees.
Teach me to turn frustration into gasoline.

Sell me on the joys of aging and disease.
Get my daughter to like whole wheat bread, lima beans, and peas.
Deny the IRS all knowledge of me.

Turn me 12 for an hour—in 7th grade again, watching, in the
     shower, bountiful Ms. Talese.
Forge my wife a necklace of the Great Chain of Being.
Let me make, at long last, the varsity make out team.

Let a certain you-know-who, you know what, and no one sees.
Teach me the one where David Copperfield turns a jumbo jet
     into a hot pastrami with pickles and Swiss cheese.
Make the trash take itself out; restore my faith in helpful mysteries.

Make Physics' laws reversible, and game scores what I think they
     should be.
Don't let my computer do bad cyber-things to me.
Grant me three wishes. No tricks, Satanic Majesty.

Train my son to step toward the pitcher, keep his weight back,
     and swing confidently.
The next time some teller at your bank chirps, "Next guest, please,"
Give me a nice meal, a strong Margarita, and a warm bed in a
     room with a fireplace, for free—

Plus honest-to-God sadness when I leave.

SUITCASE

It glares—flat-headed demon—from my shelf.
        Its airline tag's a crooked nose.
Its rivets are twin-pupiled eyes.
        Its lid, zipped shut, conceals shark teeth . . .

No, it's a passenger car on a black train.
        Four lights gleam where, unable to sleep,
four short lawyers hunch over four long briefs.
        Or it's an engine, playing "chicken"

with me, knowing that I am. Why did I buy
        a panther-black case that melds with night
and sends hope screeching up tall trees?
        If I'd picked sky-blue or tangerine,

I wouldn't see a devil's food cake, ready
        to pop open and release a vampire
who squeals, "Surprise!" I wouldn't haul
        a coal-black stone on which to sit and watch,

alone, an alien sunrise. My suitcase
        is a magic cabinet; more clothes come out
than fit inside. It's a dog I must hold tight,
        or it will leave with someone new—

a life buoy I cling to as the world floats by.
        It's a doorway to elsewhere. (Last month,
Kauai.) I open it when I arrive, to let
        scents from my old life comfort me.

Stood on one side, it's a doctor's bag;
        stood on the other, a tombstone: stark; saturnine.
It's a boulder to break toes in the dark,
        a moon-lit mesa where lost kachinas shine.

HOSPITAL

Hot spittle, sizzling on pain's grill.
Hopcycle: a gamboling bike. Hopsicle:
bouncy, tooth-chilling, bad for you.

Opposite of hope's fiddle. No
"Soldier's Joy." No "Jolie Blonde."
Losspital: place where losers

meet. Hospice: little. (How big
do death-rooms have to be?)
Hiss bottle, has pickle. Ass brittle—

like the rest of me! "Have you
ever," a clipboard-man
demands, "been hospitalized?"

Been ossified? Alphabetized?
Fossilized? Caramelized? (I won't
leave here the same, or possibly,

alive.) Hot tickle. I'm not giggling.
House pistol. If I get my hands
on one . . . Horse pizzle,

swizzle, sizzle—let me ride away!
Some guy is fishing, on TV,
for river-monsters toothier than tiger

sharks. How can I rest with all
these teeth gnawing at me?
Cords yank out every time I turn.

My monitor pings. "Sorry," I tell
the nurse who runs in. "Still
not dead." "That's good," she chirps,

and jabs a needle into me. Hiss
piddle. Hose poodle. Hat riddle:
How's a ten-gallon like a barbershop?

Cop fizzle, sop griddle, toss stipple.
Glass house-pitiful you shouldn't
throw up in, stoned or not. Hostile

hostel, I won't come back, I swear!
Hose pustule, top tickle, Oz puddle.
"Thank you," I tell each doc,

meaning, "Fuck you for being well."
Bop middle, slop griddle, rot victuals,
hope's diddle. The Grand Hotel

Oh-Well-to-Hell-with-Me.
You enter immortal, and exit disposable
as snot.

BRAIN CAMP

"Students will dissect a human brain."

Not canoeing class and campfire sing-alongs—
sawing through skulls, peeling off the dura mater,
pia mater, and arachnoid to explore the gray matter inside.

Not archery, homesickness, marshmallow-
dripping s'mores—carving out the cerebellum;
following the curves and valleys called *sulci*.

Not splitting white-skinned tribes into Arapaho,
Algonquin, Chippewa—dividing medulla from pons,
left hemisphere from right.

                   Not pulling perch
and catfish from a muddy lake with a cane pole—
dropping a line in the cerebral aqueduct; dragging up

the amygdala from limbic depths, dripping.
Not hatchets and whittling with Swiss army knives—
scalpels; bone-saws.

                   Not hobbling horses, bedding
down under the stars—lifting the tentorium cerebelli,
skirting the optic chiasma and fissure of Sylvius

to enter the substantia nigra, dark as night.
Not huddling in mummy bags, chewing dried
apricots and jerky; not dangling, tacked

to a cliff face over an abyss—bending to see
the mountains of awareness rise: the mind's range
moving off in silver mist . . .

PART II

WATERMELON

It was not a Southern watermelon that Eve took;
we know because she repented.
                    —Mark Twain

It's a green pearl the warm earth grows
around a perfect sugar grain. It's the striped egg

of the Delectosaurus, that escaped extinction
by hiding in trees till it was safe

to come down and lounge on the ground.
It's summer's jack-o'-lantern, every slice a grin.

It's a bomb full of shrapnel that boys spit
to make moms scold and sisters squeal.

Sown in a field, its helmet full of blackened teeth
gives rise to armies everyone is glad to see.

Ball-and-chain to which you're sentenced
if you're good, football which is its own field goal,

best available translation of spring rain and summer
sun, heaped high on a Hempstead truck—

it's paradise to cool your lips in one
after a hot ball game, or on a beach when, wet

from swimming, a grinning girl in a wisp
of blue bikini pleads, "Give me a bite?"

Deep in the Ozarks, Dad stopped at a roadside
stand, and bought a whole cold one, sliced

lengthwise in quarters, the four of us slurping
at our red troughs happily. "Watermelon-eater,"

as a slur, is like calling a man "big money-
maker," "fast-car driver," "bedder of beauties."

Africa's pride and greatest gift,
the watermelon inspired humans to evolve,

Egypt to civilize, and Dr. Livingstone to say,
"Nile, shmile. Find me the source of *this*."

MADE IN HEAVEN

A baby born in Sani Supra has two noses,
four eyes, two mouths hungry for milk.
Her parents—poor all their lives—grow rich
with gifts from worshippers who believe
their little Lali is Durga, three-eyed Goddess
of Valor, come to earth with a spare eye.

"Durga, make me brave," worshippers pray
as fervently as Lali's parents used to pray
for enough money to live—as, one day,
Lali will pray to find a man who loves,
not her divinity, but the single soul
that glimmers out of her four eyes—

as, elsewhere in India, "the pregnant man"
prays for a flat belly—prays people
will stop stealing glances at his private parts,
and asking, "Who's the father?"—
as, after surgery removes the twin
his body swallowed in the womb, he prays

for a friend who'll know his thoughts
before he speaks—someone
to understand and ease his many fears.
Maybe he'll go to Sani Supra,
and pray to Durga, the goddess people say
lives there.

PRAYING MANTIS ON A CHAIN-LINK FENCE

Rain that rattled through this park an hour ago
must have knocked her out of ambush in the trees.
Or was it this wind that buffets branches
too wet to grip, even with six strong hands?

Programmed to disappear by standing still,
she's unaware that, on this silver grid,
no bugs will scuttle by for her to grab,
long-limbed and quick as an NBA center;

no male will mate, then stay for dinner (hers)—
unaware she stands out like a green-bean
mustache on a snowman; like me when Nicky
Monszuk, the school bully, died in a car wreck,

and everybody else in sixth grade cried.
She'd never suspect that any passing bird
can see a meal—that, if I didn't pluck her up
and place her on a tree that she can climb

and vanish in the leaves, few boys could quell
the need to straighten out those praying arms,
and pluck from her thin neck and well-fed body
that merciless triangular green head.

FRIAR TOWHEE

It looks, with its cheerful brown eyes,
like a bird Friar Tuck, who could have been
a cardinal, but chose a cassock of dun.
My son ignores its funny hop along the concrete

wall that keeps our hill upright,
as he ignores our plum tree's flurry
of white flowers, stopped at the exact height
of the deer that forage nightly in our yard.

He's too intent on blowing up the space-
helmeted dandelions that dot our lawn.
He's more impressed by black lizards
that push-up to show blue bellies,

then, when he lunges at them, skittle away.
How could my parents hope to wow me
with the crimson fire of amaryllis, or the yellow
fanfares lilies trumpeted each spring,

when what I wanted was to chop
our backyard pines, yank pumpkinseeds
bright as serapes out of Luna Lake,
and bb-blast screaming blue jays?

The day, age 9, I found a friar flapping,
trapped in our front room where Nottingham,
our cat, crouched patiently, I didn't feel
like Robin Hood as I heaved a blanket off my bed,

and pinned poor Tuck against a wall.
Kill him, a hawk screamed, circling
in my head as I gripped the swaddled bird.
Let him go, cried crocuses and new, green leaves.

STRANGERS

"You're wet!" Mom said as I tried to slink by.
        Dad's eyes caught fire as I told how, at White Oak
Bayou Park—where, last year, a boy "disappeared"—
        a man in the restroom showed Joey, Ted, and me
his thing, and I peed my pants, rushing out of there.

Dad roared away, returning soon with Joey's dad, R.D.,
        and Ted's—"Big Ted," because he was five-three.
"Call the cops," Mom said. "Please. You'll get yourself killed."
        She gripped Dad's arm. "Dinner's getting cold . . . "
"We'll heat it up," Dad said; and we were out the door.

The restroom glowed in evening mist as we drove up.
        "Stay with Ted," Dad told me, then led R.D. inside.
A man tore from the gray brick room, just before Dad
        and R.D. dragged another out into the silver chill.
"This him?" Dad asked, meaning, *It better be.* "I think,"

I said. The man—about Dad's size—tugged feebly.
        Dad's fire-eyes flared. My goof-off dad,
who made me squeal, playing Horse Bite—who sang
        "O Holy Night" so sweetly the church ladies cried—
growled, "Sure it's him?" "I think," I said again,

and rubbed my eyes. The caught man whined
        as Dad and R.D. bulldozed him into the dark.
"Guys—I was takin' a leak, I swear," lofted back,
        then sounds like sofa-thumping, then sobs and a splash
before Dad and R.D. stalked like red-eyed zombies

from the thickening fog. "We warned him, but he felt
        like playing frog," Dad said, and everyone *har-har*ed.
Sounds bad, I know. In those days, though,
        cops told men to "take care of" molesters,
then looked away. Our dads had shot, bombed,

bayoneted Germans, Koreans, Japanese. So—
        is this poem in praise of vigilante veterans?
I'll tell you this: in six months, the "disappeared" boy
        reappeared. Turned out he'd only run away.
Nothing bad happened. Nothing he hadn't wanted done.

QUESTIONABLE

Why are Ted and Charlie prowling this dirt road as night-woods
        glower on either side?
Have they come to score some dope, or scope what's going on
        inside parked lovemobiles?
Does tomorrow's math test dampen in Ted's hand?

Is shame what makes them leave the road and crouch like toads
        as headlights scar the dark?
Is a gang fight brewing out here, where cops rarely show?
If they know it's their friend Lonnie's green Ford crunching to
        a halt,

And know Lynn Walther sits, balloon-breasts mashed against him—
        why do their guts quiver, their feet twitch to run?
Do short skirts, Fs, and nice girls' hisses make a whore?
If Lonnie asked her to a dance, why are they here?

Why, five minutes later, does Lynn screech, "Fuck you"?
When the car-door light pops on, and she flounders down the road,
        why doesn't Lonnie let her leave?
Why does he plead, "It was a joke. I'd never share you"?

Does she stop running because she thinks it's true?
"Do you see other guys?" Lonnie demands, leading her back.
        "Would I do that to you?"
What do Ted and Charlie think as they shrink and hunker low?

Will things resume inside the car?
Do Ted and Charlie, their "ten bucks apiece" in Lonnie's wallet,
        want them to?
When Lonnie's headlights lance the air and his car grinds gravel
        as it pulls away, aren't the boys glad to see it go?

HE BANGS

This is my rifle; this is my gun.
This is for killing; this is for fun.
—U.S. Marines

Strange that the smash hit "She Bangs" should pull
the train to fame for gentle William Hung,
a Berkeley engineering student whose buck teeth,

crossed eyes, and epicanthic folds shaded
by Vitalised hair would be a hate crime, chalked
on a brick wall, but make him my *Multicultural Idol.*

Alas, Judge Simon calls his voice *ghastly.*
Judge Randy looks to heaven for strength.
Judge Paula hides her face as Will gropes for the melody,

and the beat's one-two dumps him on his duff.
Why does this guy think he can sing? Well,
why does Scat Girl think her squealing makes her

Ella's heir, and not just scat? Why does
Sweater Boy believe his shimmying and bleating
will make girls throw anything but up?

Knowing you suck requires a musical ear.
Anyway, who wants to hear truth's sour blat?
Will—slapped with unanimous *Nos*—doesn't whine,

rage, beg, or cry. "I have no training at singing,"
he declares, unfazed by Simon's wry, "Impossible!"
"I gave my best, and thus have no regrets,"

the Hungster states, and marches off to be
an engineer, his good heart beneath his blue backpack,
banging.

WOE TO THE DEFEATED

"Vae victis," snarls Brennus, leader of the Celts.
He's tall, with pallid skin and eyes, his blonde mane
so stiff with sticks, leaves, and lye, he seems to stand

in a high wind, hair blown behind him like a shelf.
"Vae victis," he snarls, and heaves his heavy sword
onto the scales we've just balanced with gold,

trying to bribe him to lead his hordes away.
His face is shaved clean, but for a blonde mustache
so long it screens his chin. His Celts are many

as the acorns underneath their sacred oaks,
their war cries awful as being trepanned out of sleep,
though less bad than watching Brennus strain porridge

through that mustache. No, trepanation would be
worse, although our instruments' design will outlast
two millennia. (So say our soothsayers, at least.)

What's *really* awful is this lout telling Rome—
mouth full of mush, teeth grinding like millstones
turned by the slave that he was born to be—"Vae victis."

Oracles foresee a time when men will speak through wires,
and drive metal crates faster than any chariot—
when children will watch, on glowing boxes,

a mouse, beaver, skunk, and squirrel attend a school
where they learn to chime, "Hurray
for differences!"—not to slaughter, enslave,

or even mock the weak, but to love everyone,
like that laughingstock we crucified a few years back.
Trust me, that time is not today.

THE SAD CASE OF HISTORY

Once, he embodied objectivity: sour white
       male in a tall black hat—like a mortician
          crossed with Honest Abe.

Once, his talk was names, dates, facts
       certain as sunrise, predictable as arithmetic.
          Now he does impressions: Woman!

Black! Native American! A transsexual
       named Herstory! Now s/he ad libs, improvises,
          lies outright—a con, and proud to be.

It's sad to see him/her these days—shopping
       cart full of togas, kimonos, chain-mail suits—
          shuffling shelter to shelter, dressed in rags,

unable to hold a job or speak a definitive
       phrase—unable even to tell where
          he/she has been, or how in hell she/he got there.

AFTER THE 5-K WALK TO BEAT BREAST CANCER

Terri hauls water, diapers, and half a lemon croissant,
        in her purse big as a cotton-picker's sack, up to a table
in the shade. Tim shoves the twins' two-seated stroller
        in beside her, then goes for barbecue, as good dads do

instead of catching trout, or showering with porn stars.
        When he returns, balancing paper plates that swoon
under the sog of baked beans, cole slaw, slathered ribs,
        an old man who's been dozing, creaks to his feet.

"This table's saved," he squeaks. "You have to leave."
        The PA's blasting "I Feel Free"—a song Tim played
in high school, sure he'd be a star. Now, writer
        of manuals for espresso machines, he glares

from the old man, eyes red as a rhino's, to the dozen
        empty chairs, to Terri, who sighs, and nods, "Let's go."
"You're out of your tree," Tim says, and gnaws a rib
        until, scowling and scolding, the old man limps away.

Tim's on his third rib when a man with an ash-tray stink
        dumps himself down. "So—my grampa's out
of his tree?" Tim's rib turns tasteless, but he chews.
        "If he thinks he can save this whole table, he is."

"I'd watch your mouth, buddy, if I were you."
        He's younger, taller, heavier than Tim, but makes no move.
"If you were me, *buddy*, you'd know your grampa *is*
        out of his tree. Keep hassling us if you like pain."

"*You're* gonna give me pain? That's what you're saying?"
        Red rage drives Tim to his feet. Hawaii's out this year—
costs too much, with the kids. Each day his bad
        back hurts him more. "That's what I'm saying!"

The other guy stays down. Tim nods. "Smart choice."
    He wills his blood pressure, *Fall*. He's crowding
50. Dad was dead at 54. He wills himself to sit
        and eat until the guy lugs his tobacco stink away.

"No offense," Terri says, "but you escalated that.
    You sank to his level." "We kept our table," Tim says.
He doesn't say that, for the first time in God knows when,
        he feels raised up in his own eyes. He feels free.

THE CAT'S MEOW

For I will consider my cat . . .
—Christopher Smart

Hank plucks our window screen, and moans,
"My paws are frozen. Let me in before I die."
Even gorged on *Happy Cat*, he wails,
"Why hast thou forsaken me?"
before he bounds onto the bed, and sleeps.

Instead of, "Yay, you're back! Let me
lick you all over, then let's play," he groans,
when I come home, "I have ear mites.
And you let them *fix* me!" True, I could buy
a bird to sing, "Oh what a beautiful morning,"

(though it's really "Buzz off, other males.
Hot females, mate with me!") I could get
a hamster that chuckles, "Heh, heh, heh,
I've got cheek-pouches full of seeds, and you
don't," or a tortoise who, in a hundred

years, will never break his vow of silence.
But no, I choose my moaning cat,
who flows out of my arms like an orange river—
who springs to the top of our stone wall
easily as angels rise to heaven—who glides

with devilish grace—whose teeth and claws
are rodent death—whose fur whispers,
Caress—who, when I scratch his ears, flops
against me, gives the famous kitty grin,
and condescends to bless me with his purr.

MY SON DREAMS THAT A SHARK ATE ME

Did it leap, and pluck me off a pier?
        Did I hook the monster, and it yanked me in?
                If my son remembers, he can't say;

he fears too much to lose the friend who pitches
        Wiffle balls to him, and takes him fishing.
                Years before heart failure dragged

my father down, I dreamed that lions
        ate him, Indians scalped him, burglars
                shot him, cars ran over him. I'd wake—

night like a coffin covering me—and run
        to the front room, where Dad sat, reading.
                "I dreamed you died," I'd sob.

He'd hug me, soothe (just as I do), "You see?
        I'm fine," and give a goofy smile
                like mine as my wife leads our boy to bed.

I sit alone, my life's small lamp fighting
        to hold back—at least until he can swim
                on his own—the hungry shadows, circling.

FISHSUIT

Names are important. Ask the stars who, to protect
their kids from mediocrity, call them Moxie
Crimefighter, Audio Science, Dweezil, Hieronymus Bug.
Ask the former Daniel Michael Miller, now legally

The Dan Miller Experience. ("Call me *The*.")
Ask the man who changed his name (who knows
from what?) to Snaphappy Fishsuit Mokiligon:
a rockin', sockin', finger-poppin' joy-buzzer of a guy

who later changed Snaphappy etc. to Variable,
reminding us that life is flux; consistency,
the hobgoblin of mini-minds. That message, too,
having outlived its time, Variable asked, in 2010,

to become Fuck Censorship—a request akin
to the Walmsleys' sullen son Windigo's suggestion
that their summer cabin, "Grizzly's Den," be renamed
Pig's Wallow, Turd Corner, or Soul Cyanide,

both requests being—like Windigo's prayers
for a new job and better family, another chance
for real, limb-ripping grizzlies to roam the ever-
more-peopled, less-wooded hills—denied.

SHEEP TICKLE ME

Their thick wool—full of dirt, sticks, dung—
                  that makes their legs look toothpick-thin.
Their *baa*: its negativity made more absurd
           by quavering. The way they look in lingerie.

A deputy sheriff in Tennessee lost his job
              for stealing two sheep from a farm.
He was exposed after he threw
           one of the sheep (uncooperative? scornful?)

from the window of the Dive Rite Inn.
                When I quit college to play in a rock band,
Dad warned, "You'll end up like *him*,"
           meaning a huckster hunched by the freeway

like a shepherd grieving his sheepskins.
              Like the poor, sheep are always with us.
Six-thousand-year-old statues honor sheep.
           On the last night of 1 BC, God's Son

condescended to a manger ringed by sheep.
              The Son was called the *Lamb of God*.
Lamb of God (the band) began as *Burn the Priest*.
           A *pastor's* congregation is a *flock*.

Foolish followers are *sheep*. Women wheedle,
              "Be a lamb . . ." or "Be an angel . . ."
The angels touting Bethlehem may have been
           sheep, their choir, a harmony of bleats.

For Easter, Mom cooked leg of lamb ringed
              by worshipful spuds, mint jelly hymning
in an emerald heap. Heaven's gold streets
           need constant washing, due to sheep.

A UC Davis study failed to find lesbian sheep.
    "Since ewes solicit sex by standing still,"
said a researcher, "two may ache for one another;
        but neither they, nor we, can ever know."

CHRYSANTHEMUMS

After a day-long deluge, rain-buffed lawns, drenched
trees, and million-dollar houses stand revealed—
like Aeneas to Dido—bathed in golden light. True,

Big A sailed off later to found Rome as, left
on shore, Dido burned even their bed, and leapt
like some pro-wrestling Diva into the flames. But

isn't love worth the pain? Leander thought so.
And Juliet. And Tristan, whose name means Sadness.
Each time I saw Judy Sullivan's green eyes

and auburn hair, my brain blared "Half-Heaven,
Half-Heartache," which pretty well nails love at 17.
We know, today, how estrogen sparks testosterone

to create the lust-plus-tenderness that helps make babies,
and dads who stick around to care for them. Back then,
I called that feeling love, and worshipped it. Today,

I "love" Cajun fiddling, and Thai food, and the ranch-
style home where I live with my wife and a son
so like me, loving him is self-love. Lack of that, I guess,

made Judy down her mother's pills. Or did she love
herself too much to let envious kids call her a *slut*,
and schlumpy teachers, who should have worshipped

at her feet, fail her, which they often did?
It's years since I've wanted to die because a girl didn't
love me—or made love all night because she did.

It's years and years since I left bed at dawn to steal—
in rain, at risk of getting shot—my crazy neighbor's
head-sized, prize-winning red, yellow, and orange

chrysanthemums as offerings to a goddess in my bed.
Now, barely a block from my home, I see a kid's red-
flowered boxers billow over pants that bag to his knees

as he sprints to pluck a pink rose from someone's
garden—someone with bucks, like me. He hands
the flower to his girl. And though they have as little

chance as Orpheus had to keep Eurydice, they walk away
so close together they could be *one flesh*,
as scripture says of lovers, and we once believed.

WEBB COULD SAY LESS, MAY BE?

—from a student evaluation

But don't you think Webb's readers care
that, on a flight to Kona from LA, a blonde
in a Virgin Mary tee hulaed the length
of the airplane, nipples straining like .30-06 slugs

to pierce the shirt that, when she stretched,
bared a belly brown as crème brûlée?
Should Webb not say that such things make
his arms seem swizzle sticks in life's martini—

palm fronds in youth's trade winds—snake
tongues tasting spring air—cat whiskers
steering him through tight spaces—lobster-feelers
twitching in love's sea? Should he not say

they make him see divinity in bites of bread,
and the mouth-gouge on his red delicious apple
shaped like the inverse of Einstein's head?
Duct-tape your lips, Webb (possibly)! Botox

your tongue to make it lie like a dead skink,
a diving board so bounce-free, not one word
springs into people's ears. Be—may be?—
the hairdresser who grinds his shears to dust,

the batting champ who swings a daffodil,
the surgeon who trades his scalpel
for a butter stick. Emulate a stripper who won't,
a carpenter who saws thin air, a prophet

whose best answer is, "We'll see."
Slouch into rooms real slow, zipped lips
proclaiming, "Hey—if you're looking
for that blabbermouth Webb, don't look at me."

NADA

What a thing to call my sister: *Nada*—
Nothing, in Spanish, where *d* sounds
like *th*, Natha, two-thirds of the way

      to Nathalie where, in French, the *th*
      sounds like *t*, as in Nativity: Birth,
      the opposite of Nothing, though all

who are born return to it. Nada—the word
contagious, even Mom fizzing laughter
as she said, "Don't call your sister Nada!"

      But my gift was making fun of things.
      When Nada named her kitten *Princess*,
      I called her *Rancidia*, which stuck.

My sister's preference meant Nada.
Nada, that morphed into Nadir,
and Nodule: lump that could be cancer,

      and lead to the House of Nothing. Nada,
      of whom I sang, "doesn't have a head—
      no, not one," making Mom exclaim,

"Don't say your sister doesn't
have a head. She certainly does!"
Even my father laughed at that. Even he

      called her Nada, once—Na-Da, negation
      of Da, though he'd have died for her—
      died for Nothing and become it: nullity

Christ denied, but Buddha embraced—
zero, nil, the void, Nada, which is Heaven,
in a way. Nada: wondering why

      (I've heard) she's not much in my poems.
      Dear Nada, some say all my poems
      are about nothing. Worth it, too.

May nothing hurt you, Nada—better
than gymnast Nadia, with her perfect 10.
Decades late, I confess: I was wrong.

      The night you played Chopin in church,
      Dad got it right: "She's really something."
      Nada, who helped our parents shrink

toward death while I grew fat on life—Nada,
your virtues vast as space—you had a head;
there was nothing wrong with you.

PART III

INVISIBLE ALPACA

Stroking my son's hair, cowlicked with dreams,
　　　　and whispering, "Sorry, time for school,"
　　　　　　　　just sinks him deeper into sleep. But when I sing,

I'm an invisible alpaca; I don't make much noise.
　　　　I'm an invisible alpaca; I bite little boys,
　　　　　　　　his lip-corners twitch up. He squeals

as I give his knee the pincer-squeeze I've blamed
　　　　on alpacas since the petting zoo. "I see you, Dad!"
　　　　　　　　"I'm an alpaca," I squeak, and nip and bite

until he's up, sloshing in dawn's icy creek
　　　　that sweeps him to my car. "Be good," I warn.
　　　　　　　　"Alpaca's here." "I don't see him. Prove it!"

"Not everything real can be proved," I insist.
　　　　Too soon, my young empiricist will boot Alpaca
　　　　　　　　into Babyland where Thomas the Tank Engine,

Barney, and Fooyuck Monster already pine.
　　　　Now, with new Shaquille O'Neal high-tops,
　　　　　　　　he kicks my car door closed. "Bye Erik,"

Alpaca cries. "Bye Dad," my boy sighs, waves,
　　　　and shrugs on his backpack big as a Marine's
　　　　　　　　as my car inches forward, others shoving up

to unload their own vanishing cargo.
　　　　One last wave, then he's bouncing down
　　　　　　　　the concrete stairs as if he's riding an alpaca

on a steep trail carved by those cloud-dwelling
　　　　magicians who built Machu Picchu
　　　　　　　　and, wood flutes wailing, went invisible too.

ELIXIR

for Professor Mom

When I say my daughter transmuted my heart,
childless friends may think I'm trying
    to turn motherhood's lead weight into gold.
Jābir ibn Hayyān, eighth-century alchemist
    believed that gold was mercury plus sulfur
in perfect proportion, and that *al-iksir,*

    the philosopher's stone, would turn imperfect
metals into gold as surely as a little girl's,
    "Mommy, I don't want to let you go," can turn
an ironized brain into warm butterscotch.
    Jābir ruled chemistry for eight hundred years,
thanks to the wishful thinking that makes

    people believe in God, or god-like aliens.
Those in the movie *Forgotten* are less gods
    than devil-scientists testing human rats.
They steal a child, then try to wipe her out
    of the world's memory. (This scared
our girl so much, we had to soothe her with ice

    cream and *Rattatouille* in her bedroom.)
Forgotten's aliens can transmute anything, it seems,
    but mother-love. When that shines on,
incorruptible as gold—when Mom keeps looking
    for her girl, and won't let others forget her—
the space creeps yank their human flunkeys

back to the mothership as if they're being raised
to heaven bodily. The way they flail,
        though—like bugs in toad-tongues—doesn't
look like folks enraptured by God's love.
        Jābir's beloved mother tongue
transmuted *al* (the) plus *Ilah* (god) to Allah,

        God's One True Name. *Al-kimiya,*
the chemistry, became in English, *alchemy.*
        Al-cohol still helps us access certain gods.
Al-iksir could heal all wounds (Jābir believed)
        by balancing the body's elements.
The years I lugged a 300-pound briefcase

        labeled *Me* in my right hand, and a feather
labeled *Others* in my left, I couldn't balance
        on a rug. Now I could tightrope Grand Canyon
in a hurricane to save my child, just as ninety-
        pound women hoist 18-wheelers, and God
turned water to wine for Jesus, since the worst

        thing a host can do is to run out of food,
or subject his guests to age, disease, and death
        with no hope for salvation, no philosopher's stone
that—like Jābir, God, and the helpful aliens
        people pray for—can make everything perfect:
good as gold.

PLUMBED WINE

If Keats hadn't caught TB, if Cervantes hadn't lost
his hand in battle, if Tchaikovsky hadn't been gay . . .
—Thomas M. Cole

If, as a child, Beethoven hadn't loved
    how lead sulfate turned sour wine sweet.
        If the wine hadn't sucked the sting

out of his father's cane, his curses
    that little Ludwig was less cute
        than young Mozart, and less profitable.

If Ludwig hadn't dragged that comfort
    into adulthood. If even one doctor
        had guessed the link between plumbed

wine and the pain that doubled him—
    the ringing that, like water rushing
        into a ship's hold, drowned the sounds

of his First Symphony. If he hadn't shunned
    society, afraid someone would say,
        "Maestro, what note does that bird sing?"—

he who conducted nobles' orchestras
    and taught their children music, stripped
        of "the sense that should have been most

perfect in me"—pathetic as a blind watchman
    or armless surgeon—deaf as a wreck
        at the bottom of the sea. If isolation's

sour kiss hadn't made him a glowering
    toad, repulsing women. If he'd had
        children to love, as well as music.

If he hadn't had to carry notebooks
        to communicate, or attach a vibrating
                steel rod to his piano, then play

with the rod clamped between his teeth.
        If he hadn't thought his landlords
                poisoned him, forcing him to de-camp

like a gypsy, bowels a sea of flaming pitch,
        his only solace the music in his head,
                and plumbed wine to "stimulate

the appetite" while lead wedged, atom
        by atom, into flesh, blood, bones. If
                the "one day of perfect joy" he prayed for

hadn't beckoned with each melody,
        then dissolved in bitterness that the world
                swilled his music while he died of thirst . . .

he might not have seized on Schiller's "Ode
        to Joy," goaded to capture sounds
                that thrashed like demons—spitted, sizzling—

then rose, redeemed, to health and strength
        and victory as, seated beside the real
                conductor at the premiere of his Ninth,

he waved his arms, beat time, and brayed,
        closed eyes as useless as his ears,
                not knowing when the orchestra

had stopped until a singer, Caroline Unger,
        turned him—sick, saturnine old
                man—to face the deafening cheers.

THIRST

Thirst's tractor rumbles through the veins, harvesting dust.
Rivers evaporate. Tides of the mouth retreat. The tongue cracks,
　　baking in the body's heat.

Thirst is a trader named Sahara, offering dunes for fountains,
　　wind for shade, fire for trees.
Thirst does her striptease when you're chained to the bed,
　　whimpering, "Please . . . " .

Hunger is a marathon; thirst is a sprint. On your mark, get set,
　　die.
Who can forget chilled watermelon after a ten-mile hike, iced
　　lemonade to cool a ball game in July?

Thirsty people drink the sea. They drink their own or others' pee.
They drink oil, wood chips, pumice, molten rock . . .
Rise slowly from the depths of thirst, or else your cells, like the air
　　bladders of deep-sea fish, will pop.

Thirst is a sand sandwich, a griddle shirt, boulder golf ball, stingray
　　back-scratcher, rattlesnake toothbrush.
Thirst's tarantula comes crawling, crawling . . .

A man without drink is a tree without wood, a lie without faking,
　　a breeze without air.
A woman without drink is a boat without floating, a door without
　　exit, a chair without a place to park your rear.

Thirst for power, knowledge, love, salvation, victory, artistic
　　excellence—fatal, each one.
Dr. Pepper is the friendly hello mellow from the land of sky blue
　　yahoo Mountain it's the real thing Coke.

Hey-oh-ah, hey-oh-ah, Thirst's warriors are dancing.
  Hey-oh-ah, prayers arrow into the sun's eye.
Hey-oh-ah, vanished deer and buffalo can't save the people.
  Hey-oh-ah, hey-oh-ah, the drought rains down.

CHELONIAN RHAPSODY

If some accident of evolution had led reptiles
to develop a neocortex while maintaining their
nonexistent child-rearing habits, they might
have ended up writing powerful verse about
some other deep-seated biological urge—
temperature regulating, say.
            —*Discover Magazine*

To drag out of my burrow on a cloudy day,
          barely warmth enough inside my shell
to burn the fat that fuels my limbs, stiff
          as logs from sunless sleep. To spy a gap

between the trees, and watch space-time
          flow until the clouds crack open,
and the sun swims free. To feel its fire
          bake down, making my shell glow,

my brain become a sun that simmers
          like the fusion-farms where we raise
snails, worms, lettuce, grapes. To let
          June heat swell in me like the urge

to mate when a high-shelled beauty
          drags by, urine-scent sweeter
than dewberries in rain—to feel
          that heat, which powers flight between

the stars, return me to the time when Old
          Turtle worshipped the sun, before
we learned the science of eternal life,
          shoved lesser beings off extinction's

cliff, and owned the world—alone
  with the machines we build for company.
To let solar winds fan me into a flame
  of praise, then, drawn to some pond's

sheen, let my legs swim me down
  as in the ancient, hibernating days,
dark waters closing like my birth-egg
  around my dimming dreams.

INTROSPECTION AFTER *FEAR FACTOR*

Admit you'd freak if forced to cross a chasm
on wires that wobble and sag in saw-toothed winds
as, each ten thigh-quivering feet, you squat

and grab a yellow flag. Could anything induce you
to chew duck embryos and cockroaches,
then wash them down with liquified pig spleen?

You'd have to be dead to let bees, scorpions,
or tarantulas swarm over you. True,
the blonde Surfer Girl—diamond stud lighting

the flat beach of her belly as she's locked
in a glass coffin and sunk in an icy lake—fears
her bikini will release a corkscrew hair.

Bartender-Bodybuilder, grinning through a mask
of bees, fears he's a bit underdeveloped
you-know-where. Haw-hawing Cowboy,

who giddyups off with the 50,000-buck prize,
would scoop out and swallow his own eyes
before he'd read an ad, much less a page of Keats.

M. Artiste, though, battles the shakes each time
he parks downtown at night, speaks to a pretty
grocery clerk, or books his own flight on the Internet.

While some men develop strength, endurance,
mastery of pain, he exercises sensitivity. Result?
He sees disasters whiz like meteors at his body's

frail capsule. Result? Life strikes him as quick breaths
seized between tsunamis—rare apple martinis
amid snifters of pig spleen piled high and deep.

Result? His longest escape from fear comes
in the moments between the shark tank of sex
and the blood-drenched, haunted house of sleep.

HAUNTED

Mom Hosts Haunted House in Home Where Children Died.
—KTLA News

The giant—nine feet tall; claw-fingers
dripping blood—lunges. We scream,
leap back like stomped water,
then slosh forward as he blomps away.

"How'd they do this?" people say,
meaning make the house look authentically
burned: charred boards, collapsed roof,
floors black as eggs forgotten on the stove.

The man who, as he chats with guests,
melts into a skeleton, looks real. So does
the corpse who—organs oozing, shimmery
with worms—grins from his autopsy table,

Zombie heads with hot-coal eyes
surprise two teenaged girls, who stampede
with ecstatic shrieks beneath the Green-Glow
EXIT sign. Plunging through webs

twitchy with tarantulas, they burst outside,
where a witch clunks Milky Ways
into their sacks, a warty mask hiding
the face that, just last year, was hideous

with helplessness to save her boys
when their heater—bought to keep them
snug—lit the drapes she'd hung to help them
sleep. Only the neighbors know

why two small gravestones hog the whole
front yard, and why the actor
in the giant suit takes care, in his stilt-high
stumblings, not to knock them down.

WATCH FOR DWARFS,

a sign on the Black Forest Highway states
as little men with shouldered picks scurry
behind a curvy girl who must be *Schneewittchen*:
"Snow White." Insensitive? Possibly—
yet an improvement on *ARBEIT MACHT FREI.*

Watch for Dwarfs could have helped me
when, after a long day of Freud and Jung
at USC, I checked my mirror, backed out
of my parking space, heard a screech, then saw
a motorized wheelchair whip from my wake,

a raging Rumpelstiltskin at the helm.
"Watch where you're going, cocksucker son
of a bitch!" he shrieked by way of introduction.
He had more on his mind, and voiced it
as I yelled, "Sorry," and burned away

too fast, I hoped, for him to read my license plate.
On campus, most wheelchairs flew tall red
warning flags to cross the automotive seas.
But why should the differently abled
make things easier for me? How dare I think,

"That goblin could have wrecked my life"—
my academic galleon dashed on the reefs
of lawsuits, jail, bankruptcy,
my high and gleaming aspirations sunk?
I should have felt guilty. Instead, like the time

I shoplifted *Fanny Hill,* then hid (I swear)
in a doghouse while juvie hall, parental vengeance,
and eternal embarrassment banged by,
I felt blessed in my escape. When, years
later, Dr. Lichtman pulled from between

my wife's gory thighs a tiny, orange
humanoid—point-headed, fish-slippery—
I asked, shaking with dread, "Is he a dwarf?"
As if that raging little man had finally found,
and taken his revenge on me.

BEAUTY MARK

Wedged underneath Stan's widow's peak,
it's a brown boulder poised to fall and crush his nose.
It's a slow-motion bullet to his brain—
an unexploded cancer bomb—a ship-gutting rock
that juts from a pale, wrinkled sea.

Like Navajos who let Grandmother Spider share their homes,
does he respect the mole's right to be
loathsome? Does he think it lends *character*
to his hangdog mug? Is he imprisoned by the male mentality
that calls cosmetic concerns *pussified*?

Is the thing a wit? A sorcerer? A seer?
Has he insured it? Set up its college fund?
What gall to gripe, *I can't get laid*,
with that turn-off knob shadowing his bed.
"I don't trust it," one woman told me. "Too well-fed."

It's a great conversation piece—when *he* can't hear.
(Who'd dare ask, "How's it hangin'?" when he's near?)
Sometimes I fear it's speaking straight to me:
You bedded Pam, and never called.
You let Mom die miserably in a nursing home.

I stay as far away as I can get,
as if it might leap onto my chin, and burn,
or hiss, "I see you when you think you're most alone."
As if its small cask holds the secret grief
to which my heart, that hopeless drunk, always returns.

THE WISH TO JUMP IN A CAR AND JUST DRIVE

is like the wish to just keep eating, just keep
surfing, just keep dancing, playing baseball,
making love, watching the sun squeeze

from behind mauve mountains as a trophy trout
tail-walks across a lake that would be
agate-smooth, except for splashing fish.

The wish comes, naturally, when times are bad—
to get away, to start again, to leave the ground
we've over-farmed, the worn-out house,

the lover time has mummified. But it comes,
too, when good things lock us up too tight—
the wish to shut the car door softly, turn

the key and back out fast, not checking
the mirror until we're bound . . . somewhere.
Too soon, I'll have to stop for food, gas,

restroom, or just rest. Money will run out.
The road will end. Still, for a while,
I'm leaping—silver-winged and slippery-quick—

out of the sea, slicing through bright, salty air
while famished tuna churn the ocean's gloss
to red froth, way down there.

THE BEST PART OF THE DAY

Soggy summer evenings as the ball game
gleaks and *squarwks* from his Range
Rider Radio—as Jannie scolds her dolls,

Mom clinks dishes, and Dad sets his yodeling
laugh free, Howie glops Neat's-Foot Oil
onto his K-Mart glove, kneads

and pounds the oil into the leather,
jams a nicked brown ball into the pocket,
and rubber-bands the whole thing shut.

Some day he'll wax his *pre-owned* Ford
with the same care; manicure his scrap
of lawn; mash egg salad for his daughter's

lunch; unsnarl his toddler's tawny hair.
Tomorrow, though, at Dad's Club Field,
he'll watch a pop-up plop three feet

from where he sprawls as if hit by a truck.
He'll see Bobby Saylor whack another one
into the trees, and Chan Washington flame

fastballs past kids like him, who freeze,
or dive for cover as the umpire quacks,
"Streek Three." He'll ride home in Mom's

DeSoto, bringing, win or lose, no thrill
of victory. Still, that night—scrubbed
clean, thin legs crossed Indian-style

on Nolan Ryan sheets—oil in hand,
glove in lap, Astros on the Range Rider,
there he'll be.

AT 5 A.M., THE ONLY SOUNDS

that leak into this mountain cabin
come from birds. Chirps flutter
through my window from the shadowed

trees. Something *cluck-clucks*.
Something else elaborates on Woody
Woodpecker's *hu-hu-hu-WA-ho* theme.

Tall pines stand ready to keep me
company, though needles and a certain
sappiness impede our closeness. Still,

I feel transcendental, making do
with a non-Posturpedic bed. If I chop
firewood, and lotus down as the stove's

heat massages me, maybe the thoughts
market projections scare away
will creep toward me like chipmunks

with quick, flicking tails, scuffling
paws, quizzical eyes. Maybe
my heart will fly back from wherever

it fled when adulthood's comet
cratered me. I'll embrace solitude
like a faithful wife. I'll kneel

and worship self-sufficiency.
I'll shoulder that shovel by the snow-
door, and dig out the true me . . .

But now, across the woods, above
the yak of jays, and the whispers-
behind-my-back of evergreens,

I hear a sneeze—undeniably human,
with its mix of relish and apology.
"God bless you," I can't help but say.

THANK YOU, CAROL WHITE

for selling, at just $19.95, the Infinity Razor (guaranteed
forever), and for throwing in, from sheer goodwill,
a finger-shaped Nose-Hair Trimmer. Dear Carol White
who, for a paltry sixteen bucks, will send Granny
a "Flannel Duster" with plaid Peter Pan collar designed

to stop Age in its tottering tracks—this same Carol
White has slashed the price of Pull My Finger Farting
Santas—for which competitors gouge twenty-plus—
to a merry $13.95. Now every family can have one
(two if they like) to spew, "Ah, the Holiday smells,"

and make Grampa shake like those bowls of cherry Jell-O
served in the best hospices. Thank you, Carol White,
for Arch Easers, and Stay-Dry Waterproof Undies,
and Hair-Cutting Umbrellas (save hundreds on barbers!),
and Toe Straighteners, and Tub-Transfer Chairs.

Thanks for Support Hose and Extra-Loud Alarm Clocks
and Ring Cuddlers to hold your sparklies on tight
as flesh wastes away. Thanks for Sonic Mole Chasers,
and Door-Wedge Alarms to stop intruders and give them
heart attacks, and Mold No More, which no home,

Retirement or not, should be without. Thanks for Jumbo
Lint Removers, Pie Crust Shields, Electric Card Shufflers
(when fingers lose that Vegas snap), and the Fishing Pen,
which telescopes into a three-foot rod so that busy execs
can land dinner as they ink their million-dollar deals.

Special thanks, though, on this Christmas Eve (which
could be anybody's last) for Farting Santa. So what
you weren't a cheerleader, and got nixed by Yale?
You married badly, never made manager, raised psycho kids,
weren't well or even moderately liked? It's not too late!

Just as shepherds, wise men, and donkeys praised a savior
who passed gas sweet as honeydew, folks will praise you
for the gift of laughter: one heartfelt *Ho! Ho! Ho!*
better than mountains of gold, frankincense, myrrh—
a taste of heaven, before we have to go.

STOWAWAY

In movies, when the killer is trapped
in a snapshot—"rabbi" sweating blood
behind the ice swan; sniping "jogger"
bisecting baby's toddle in the park—
Herr Hit-man has to track the shutterbug,
and retake the film at any price.

Many a tourist's Nikon and/or skull
has been smashed by a snarling stranger
as some guilty love shrinks from the light.
I, though, am thrilled if someone's
victory toast contains a shot of me.
In albums worldwide, I'm proud

to be grabbing my trick knee,
spilling cherry soda on my vest,
or simply waving with the rest
as bride and groom set sail,
a topless clogger rocks the boardwalk,
or somebody's kindergarten Angel

takes a big Little League swing.
The camera reaches at light speed
across ball park or beach to steal
what I'd pay it to take from me.
My books may all fall out of print,
my name be lost with every story linked

to it—the Killer Shrimp defenestration;
my face shocked by the cow-pasture
cannoneer. Yet, in flat rectangles snatched
from the world's four-dimensional froth,
my form survives. Kilroy only attended;
I was here.

CELESTE

Strange, the bits of memory that rise.
    —Clare Cook

Love for my son chains me to my desk, December 21,
fighting to finalize my grades so I can play Santa for him,
when—startling as virgin birth—an e-mail flashes in:

    Clare Cook seeks my ex-wife, Jillian. "You had
    a turtle named Pismyra," she writes. (To prove
    she's no humbug?) "We fed the Lake Washington ducks."

I feel like Scrooge, besieged by ghosts: young Me,
Pismyra, flailing in my hand; Jillie, laughing,
tossing "crackers to quackers" from my inflatable boat . . .

    "J and I split up. She lives in Maui, last I heard.
    Good luck," I type, and hunker hard over my grades.
    A kid with perfect attendance bombed his final

because the meds that keep him from jumping off a bridge
have cluster-bombed his memory . . . *Blink, blink,*
blink, blink, blink: Clare is back. "You had a one-

    man band, and sang a Gene Pitney song to me.
    My heart was all aflutter," she writes, with no apparent
    irony. "I thought you and Jillie were magic."

One-man band sounds like some clown, hot-water-bottle
tubas in both arms, stomping a drum while kazooing
"Toot Toot Tootsie." Still—Shazam!—my ghost

    is crooning, "Only Love Can Break a Heart."
    I'd listen longer, but I need to speed up Santa's sleigh,
    and still not crash my student's prospects with an F,

or cheat his classmates by giving him a grade he didn't
(is this justice, kindness, or sentimentality?) earn. Now
here's a woman, married twenty years, whose heart I never

>knew fluttered for me in a time that—like my parents'
>perfect harmony on "Silent Night," the red satin angel
>that topped our tree, the magic between Jillian and me—

I can't bring back except (be still my fluttering heart)
in memory. "Your blow-up boat's name," Clare reminds me,
"was *Celeste*."

APPROACHING POETRY

> I'm terrified to approach poetry.
> —English teacher, Hoover High

Try watching her reflection in your mirror
as you back toward her in an armored car.
Expect your heart to blorp and splutter. Don't

expect she'll be alone. Her dance card
is always full. Her phone is always busy.
Even if she had Call Waiting, she wouldn't make

anyone wait for *you*. Then there's her dad:
Godzilla without the sense of humor, roaring
questions hot as brimstone: "How will you

support her? What Authority declares you worthy
to lick the ground beneath her Pyrrhic feet?"
And there's her agent, fur hat wide as a flying

saucer, enough pinkie-ice to sink the Titanic,
and a blade for slicing epic egos down to size.
Your only hope is, she wants to be understood.

Drop in after midnight, if you dare. Wear clothes
you feel comfortable in. Comb your hair
the way you like it. Walk right up and ring her bell.

If you're a fake, her dad will make you take a job
in deconstruction; her agent will beat a confessional
sonnet out of you. But if you're lucky,

and your heart is true, she'll meet you at the door
in baby-doll pajamas. Let her cook your favorite foods.
Wolf 'em down. You won't get fat.

Don't say you love her; everyone says that.
She'll try to lead you to her bedroom, but don't go.
Say you want to get to know her first.

THAT THING

> Shake that thing.
> —Wynonie Harris

Rake that thing into the fire. Watch it burn with a green flame.
Break that thing in two pieces, one for me, one to feed the land
    crabs clacking at your knees.

Fake that thing into the air, drive to the hoop, lay the ball onto
    the glass, and save the game. Pretty please.
Cake that thing with so much medicated goop that sags and
    wrinkles disappear, and once again it's sweet 16.

Cook that thing into a cobbler. Sprinkle with nutmeg and rue.
    Bake until it glows fluorescent blue,
Take that thing to Hawaii. Let it tutor you in hula, scrub failure's
    eggnog off your mug, and mend your brain if a bad
    coconut descends.

Wake that thing by yelling, "Come on, guys! We're here!" Drag it
    off the bus and make it run, flip-flops flapping, into the
    warm-as-a-bathtub Bay of Things You Used to Love, But
    Now You Fear.
Make that thing sit up, roll over, and declare your worth when
    the world stamps REDUCED FOR QUICK SALE on
    your bum. Change it into an ottoman, an otter, an
    autoharp, an auto which is a harp too, and plays more
    angelically, the closer to light's speed you go.

Chase that thing back to wherever such things grow. Revel in
    the Day-Glo orange trees and orchid-air; sip from the
    steel-gray stream that makes you stronger than the Hulk;
    more iron-jawed than Superman; able to tell a joke so
    everybody laughs, instead of wishing you'd step on a
    land mine.
Mace that thing, and throw it in The Hole. Whine as you will, it
    can't do much more for you, now.

Better to take up golf or bridge, chess in the park, or
        shuffleboard. Better to join an opera club and go on
        cruises where you never leave the ship, and buy the
        grandkids dolls with grass skirts they'll rip off, and find
        smooth plastic underneath. Better leave moving,
        grooving, being delicately crude to sweet young dingbats
        like we were when, to such wondrous effect, you'd
Shake for me that thing I loved so much: that much-loved thing.

TO RAISE MY GHOST

for K

Think of me wading in a free-stone creek.
Think dawn, minutes before sun slaps the water green.

Mount my floppy anti-cancer hat on me.
Add the camouflage waders I bought half-price, my khaki fishing
        vest,

Plus clip-on shades and a jack-o'-lantern grin.
My rod should be clamped under my right arm, orange fly line
        bellying.

Let algaed stones shine gold in shallows that merge into a shore
        of salt-white boulders sprinkled under shadowed cliffs.
In my hands, let me hold—without squeezing—a two-foot rainbow
        trout.

The yellow, black, and red spots on its silver-flank-with-one-pink-
        stripe will mimic perfectly the play of light on rocks
beneath the water where I'll place the fish; then we'll both flash
        away.

THE GOOD SURVIVES

Not the time Jane threw a coffeepot at Don,
but the time they swam with turtles in Puako Bay.

      Not getting drunk and crashing your friend's car,
      but handing him your #20 Adams, that's caught fish all day.

Not the father's snarl and hissing belt—
the time he played catch for an hour, sick with flu.

      Einstein intuited this law, but couldn't prove it:
      Not his mad son and ruined marriage—$E = mc^2$.

Not Colly Cibber—Dryden, Swift, and Pope.
Not *Sweet Rebel Sword*—*Moby Dick*.

      If not in heaven, then in mind, Auschwitz evaporates;
      the orchid's purple stays. Not the boy drowned

in a backyard pool, the girl's heart missing beats,
then lying still. The way she'd lift her arms up

      from her crib, and say, "Kiss. Kiss." The way he'd throw
      open the bedroom door, and say, "Daddy, it's day."

ACKNOWLEDGMENTS

The author would like to thank the editors of the following pub-
lications for first publishing these poems, sometimes with other
titles and in other versions:

Asheville Poetry Review: "Plumbed Wine," "Winter Song"; *Atlanta
Review*: "Invisible Alpaca," "Watermelon," "Why Are People So
Mean?"; *Barrow Street*: "Stowaway," "The Sad Case of History";
Birmingham Poetry Review: "The Best Part of the Day," "*Webb
Could Say Less, May Be?*"; *Boulevard*: "Explanations"; *Bryant
Literary Review*: "Dedication," "My Son Dreams That a Shark Ate
Me"; *Carbon Copy*: "He Bangs," "Introspection after *Fear Factor*";
Chariton Review: "The Good Survives," "Use Of Force"; *Chiron
Review*: "After the 5-K Walk to Beat Breast Cancer"; *Cimarron
Review*: "Haunted," "Questionable"; *Cincinnati Poetry Review*:
"Suitcase"; *Ecotone*: "Chelonian Rhapsody," "Praying Mantis
on a Chain-Link Fence"; *Evansville Review*: "Strangers"; *5 AM*:
"Breathalyzer," "*Watch for Dwarfs*"; *Great River Review*: "At 5
A.M., the Only Sounds"; *Green Mountains Review*: "Approaching
Poetry," "Elixir, "Made in Heaven," "Thanks Again"; *Greensboro
Review*: "Moth," "The Wish to Jump in a Car and Just Drive"; *Gulf
Coast*: "Things We Know"; *Harvard Review Online*: "That Thing";
Hunger Mountain: "To Raise My Ghost"; *Iron Horse Literary Review*:
"Celeste"; *Michigan Quarterly Review*: "Chrysanthemums"; *Nerve
Cowboy*: "American Dream," "Beauty Mark"; *Pearl*: "Thank You,
Carol White"; *Ploughshares*: "Nada"; *Poetry International:* "Thirst";
Prairie Schooner: "Dairy Farm," "The Cat's Meow"; *River Styx*:
"Sheep Tickle Me"; *Southeast Review*: "Fishsuit," "How Can I Exceed
Your Expectations?"; *Subtropics*: "Friar Towhee"; *Tampa Review*:
"Postmodernism Missed the Opry"; *Tin House*: "Someone Else's
Life"; *Zocalo Public Square*: "In the Face, Hard."

"Woe to the Defeated" first appeared in *Bat City Review.*

"Brain Camp" first appeared in *North American Review.*

"Respect" was first published in the *Paris Review* (issue 194, fall
2010).

"Hospital" was first published in *Slate Magazine* (www.slate.com).

The writing of this book was partially funded by California State University, Long Beach, Scholarly and Creative Activities Awards.

Special thanks to, alphabetically, Laurence Goldstein, Ron Koertge, Ed Ochester, Karen Schneider, and William Trowbridge for invaluable editorial assistance, and to Edward Hirsch, who got the train on track.

www.ingramcontent.com/pod-product-compliance
Lightning Source LLC
Chambersburg PA
CBHW022335191225
37080CB00020B/886